NOT BY
ACCIDENT

NOT BY ACCIDENT

WHAT I LEARNED
FROM MY SON'S
UNTIMELY DEATH

Isabel Fleece

MOODY PRESS
CHICAGO

ISBN: 0-8024-6583-8

1 3 5 7 9 10 8 6 4 2

Printed in the United States of America

F o r e w o r d

THE CHAPTERS OF
Not by Accident are like windows through which we can see the reactions of a Christian mother's heart to the sovereign overruling of God in a time of intense human sorrow and suffering. The book is divided into two parts—God and Ned. In the first section, the author shows how real and restful is a faith that trusts the God who never makes a mistake; the God who rather causes all things to work together for our good and His glory. The second division is devoted to a motherly yet masterful appreciation of a boy's life before his unexpected home-call.

Throughout these pages, there are eternal principles to be seen, deep lessons to be learned, and much comfort to be derived. Essentially, however, *Not by Accident* is a reflection of a quality of life rarely found these days in the Christian church. It is one thing to preach the crucified life; it is another to live such a life. But I can say that Mrs. Fleece and her husband both preach and live this life, which issues from the deepest identification with Christ and His cross. Their very sorrow and suffering were but an opportunity to demonstrate the truth of George MacDonald's words that "the Son of God suffered unto death, not that men might not suffer, but that their sufferings might be like His." In the hour of trial the life of Christ was magnified in their mortal bodies. Ned's cousin, Katherine, who escaped unscathed when the seeming tragedy occurred, testifies to this fact. She wrote:

> *Immediately after the accident, I kept wondering, "What will Aunt Isabel and Uncle Allen say when they hear about Ned? How will they take it? How will they feel about the fact that I was spared and Ned taken?"*
>
> *Then Uncle Allen walked into the room where I was and, although he appeared pale and shaken, there was an expression of peace on his face that was different from anything I have ever seen. He looked at me with concern and love, and asked, "Katherine, are you all right?" His thoughtfulness at such a time touched my heart.*
>
> *Later I learned of the wonderful way all the family received the news of Ned's death, and of Ned's own feeling toward death, and I came to know in a new way what it means to be truly saved. Above all, I wanted to belong to the Lord and to have a personal knowledge of His presence. I knew that He was speaking to my heart, and that He had spared me for a definite purpose. At this time I surrendered my life to Him, and it is my prayer that He will use me for His glory.*

To my mind such a tribute is the final test of genuine Christianity—for Christianity has been defined as "the ability to react in all situations as Christ would react." And this is what we see here. If you would know the secret, then thoughtfully and prayerfully peruse these pages.

STEPHEN F. OLFORD

Part One

GOD

Prologue

GOD IN HIS MERCY

was pleased to call into His presence our youngest son, Ned, in June 1960, in an automobile accident. Since that time my heart has been strangely stirred to tell others how the Lord held us to Himself in loving embrace and brought us peace.

Our family was vacationing at the beach. Ned, with a newly acquired driver's license, wanted to run all the errands, and we let him when possible. On that occasion, though I could have gone myself, I had him take his younger cousin to her house to get her swimming suit. It was a simple thing—a short trip on an island road that seemed safe from danger.

However, God's plan was above my plan. The trip was interrupted, and Ned was in heaven.

At that point, there was much for me to learn. And somehow writing it down has made the learning clearer. At the time of the accident there were many questions: "How did it happen?" "Where did it happen?" "Why did it happen?" As each question slapped my aching consciousness, my heart cried out its only answer: The circumstances that surround an accident are insignificant to a child of God; but the God who surrounds the circumstances is infinite.

One

I LEARNED . . .

that God is good and that all things work together for good to them that love Him.

In that first moment, when word came that there had been an accident—a bad accident—we knelt in anguished prayer. I could only say, "Lord, let it be good for everyone concerned. Let it be as good, Lord, as it can possibly be." And it was. Before I called He answered. It was good for Ned: He went immediately to be with Christ. It was good for Katherine, his eleven-year-old cousin who rode with him: She was not seriously injured. There was no other car or person involved, and that was good. And then, strangely, it was good for us. For in the eternal greatness of our Father's love this is one of the "all things" that is working together for our good.

"Oh how great is thy goodness, which thou hast laid up for them that fear thee" (Psalm 31:19).

Two

I LEARNED . . .

that God is fully trustworthy and that in the vast realm of His knowledge and wisdom there is no room for the faithless question, "Why?" With God there is no "if." *If* I had not sent Ned on the errand, *if* we had not let him have his driver's license, *if* we had never gone to the beach, *if* he had only gone elsewhere for the summer as he had once considered. An endless line of "ifs" could stretch before us—an "if" for every moment of our lives. *If* we had only done it differently. But up above each "if" and beyond each finite thought stands One who is the eternal God, and from the realm of His abode He sees the end from the beginning and charts the course that leads us. His purposes are sure, His will absolute, His foreknowledge supreme. Before the foundation of the world His plan was made, and no unexpected accident has ever taken Him by surprise. His hand—His loving and almighty hand—was in control of that car that day. And when the sixteen years of Ned's bright life on earth were completed, God took him home where now a brighter life has begun.

"O the depth of the riches both of the wisdom and knowledge of God! how unsearchable are his judgments, and his ways past finding out!" (Romans 11:33).

Three

I LEARNED . . .

that all the things I have believed are true. Since becoming a Christian years ago, I have believed in the Bible—that it is the inspired, holy Word of God, and that God has not harbored any error in its pages. I have read the Word and trusted it. I have had no doubts concerning God and Christ, His blessed Son and our Savior. I have stood in this same place with many heartsick souls and read to them the Word of God and prayed, believing God when He said, "My grace is sufficient" (2 Corinthians 12:9), and trusting Him to fulfill His Word when He said, "I will never leave thee, nor forsake thee" (Hebrews 13:5); "Let not your heart be troubled, neither let it be afraid" (John 14:27). John 15:26 speaks of the Comforter, "whom I will send unto you from the Father, even the Spirit of truth."

But in the hours that followed Ned's call home, I suddenly and silently found an awakening within my soul that declared that all the things I had believed true, were true. The silence of eternity crept upon my waiting soul, and I was stilled before its limitless ages. Time rolled before me in its endless sea, and my soul moved to touch the fringes of the firmament, while my being bowed in quiet reverence to the greatness of God.

God seemed not far away but near, and in His mercy and faithfulness He reached across the universe to touch my life that I might acknowledge the magnitude of His power. All that God is overcame the little that man is, and my spirit was released into the infinite ways of the almighty One.

> *Whither shall I go from thy spirit? or whither shall I flee from thy presence? If I ascend up into heaven, thou art there: if I make my bed in hell, behold, thou art there. If I take the wings of the morning, and dwell in the uttermost parts of the sea; even there shall thy hand lead me, and thy right hand shall hold me.* (Psalm 139:7–10)

There was no psychological release of prayer that somehow vaguely stilled my heart that day. Let scientists sneer, agnostic souls contemptuously lay their man-made claims to peace of mind through the universal tuning of their spirits to the meter of transcending thought. My hope was "built on nothing less than Jesus' blood and righteousness"; and in that hour of my great need all the power of heaven was ready at God's command. A supernatural summons from the throne of God let angels speed their way to minister by my side, and the Holy Spirit came and comforted me.

Four

I LEARNED . . .

that the Word of God is an anchor to the soul, and to flee to it is to find strong consolation from God. As the hours dragged their weary way across the stillness of that first night, it seemed as if time had ceased, and we were held suspended in deep despair. No rest or sleep, no quietness or light— nothing but the deep, deep pain—nothing but that and God. As our senses began to take in what had happened, and we began to believe that Ned was gone, I closed my eyes and asked for help. And the great Lover of our souls, our blessed Savior who is Himself the Eternal Word, poured into my listening heart the sweetness of the Word of God, and I was quickened. It was my comfort in affliction, and each soothing sentence became sweet to my taste. I did not take a Bible in my hands and read it, but I lay in quietness and listened. And it was as though Jesus Himself drew near and spoke to me, for my mind pored over verse after verse.

The Shepherd's Psalm was there, and as I walked through the strange valley of the shadow of death I knew the comfort of His rod and His staff.

The Holy Spirit took the things of Christ and showed them to me: "I am the resurrection, and the life"—this verse is underlined in Ned's Bible—"he that believeth in me, though he were dead, yet shall he live: and whosoever liveth and believeth in me shall never die" (John 11:25–26).

Peace I leave with you, my peace I give unto you: not as the world giveth, give I unto you. Let not your heart be troubled, neither let it be afraid. (John 14:27)

The Spirit itself beareth witness with our spirit, that we are the children of God: and if children, then heirs; heirs of God, and joint-heirs with Christ; if so be that we suffer with him, that we may be also glorified together. (Romans 8:16–17)

God shall wipe away all tears from their eyes; and there shall be no more death, neither sorrow, nor crying, neither shall there be any more pain: for the former things are passed away. (Revelation 21:4)

Come unto me, all ye that labour and are heavy laden, and I will give you rest. (Matthew 11:28)

In all their affliction he was afflicted, and the angel of his presence saved them. (Isaiah 63:9)

For hours the gentle voice of the indwelling Christ brought healing to my soul, and I was stilled. There is a balm in Gilead; there is a Physician there (see Jeremiah 8:22). "He sent his word, and healed them" (Psalm 107:20).

Five

I LEARNED . . .

that to trust God is to trust His way, not mine. I came to realize that my intended way is made by human plans and therefore faulty in its principle and frail in its exercise. But as for God, His way is perfect. On the day of Ned's death, I asked God for protecting care, and I believed Him for it.

Through the years I had read Psalm 91 many times and applied its glorious truths to our family's needs. In the safety of our home we had seen our children grow before the Lord and become His own. And as they went out into the world, we did not fear that they were doing evil, but we constantly prayed lest they be tempted, and we had the assurance from the Lord that greater was He that was in them than he that was in the world (1 John 4:4). We sought the Lord that they would not be tempted above that which they were able to bear (1 Corinthians 10:13). And as they went about the various activities of their lives, our prayer was unceasing that they would be kept from evil and that the Lord would preserve their going out and their coming in (Psalm 121:7–8). The promises of God ever rang within my listening heart: "Because thou hast made the Lord, which is my refuge, even the most High, thy habitation; there shall no evil befall thee, neither shall any plague come nigh thy dwelling. For he shall give his angels charge over thee, to keep thee in all thy ways" (Psalm 91:9–11).

What happened on June 21 at five P.M.? Ned left with joy to do what I asked. He wasn't far from home; he wasn't speeding. Where were the angels who had charge over him that day, and why did they not bear him up? Had God forgotten His promise? Was my trust misplaced, my faith in vain? Oh, blessed answer straight from the heart of God: "He that dwelleth in the secret place of the most High shall abide under the shadow of the Almighty" (Psalm 91:1). "The angel of the Lord encampeth round about them that fear him" (Psalm 34:7).

The angels were there that afternoon—only this time they were sent from the throne of God on an errand of mysterious importance. The Lord Jesus leaned from the battlements of heaven, opened a door, called a name, and waited while the angels bore into His presence our young son. Ned had been accident-prone. He was constantly getting hurt—or nearly so—and always before he had come through all right. But this time the curve, the threat of an oncoming car over the center line, a sudden wrench of the wheel, a sand pocket on the shoulder, the overturn of the car, and Ned was gone. God's purposes are sure. There were more angels with Ned that moment than there had ever been before. There were the angels who took care of Katherine and kept her from injury, scar, or death. And there were other angels who had, I feel, a sacred privilege, for they carried Ned and presented him before the throne. I wonder if, as he suddenly stood before his Savior, he did not say, "How do you do, Sir? I am Ned." And I am sure the welcoming smile that greeted him banished all fear, all strangeness, and all questions. I can only imagine this scene; but I wait with longing for that time when I too will be there, and Ned will tell me about it.

> For thou hast delivered my soul from death, mine eyes from tears, and my feet from falling. I will walk before the Lord in the land of the living. (Psalm 116:8–9)

> The Lord is my strength and song, and is become my salvation. . . . I shall not die, but live, and declare the words of the Lord. . . . Open to me the gates of righteousness: I will go into them, and I will praise the Lord: This gate of the Lord, into which the righteous shall enter. (Psalm 118:14, 17, 19–20)

> The Lord shall preserve thee from all evil: he shall preserve thy soul. (Psalm 121:7)

> Father, I will that they also, whom thou hast given me, be with me where I am; that they may behold my glory, which thou hast given me. (John 17:24)

The Lord opened a gate and bade His child, clothed in His own righteousness, to enter in. He asked that Ned, one of those the Father had given Him, be with Him where He is to behold His glory.

Who am I, that I would say no to Him? Or what am I that I would keep from that blest Presence this one I love so well? Ned—our Ned, closely cropped hair and crooked smile—in that glory. His heart at rest, his journey done. His last enemy conquered. He does not have yet to die!

Yes, God was in control that day, and the angelic hosts were there to carry out the perfect will of a loving heavenly Father.

Six

I LEARNED . . .

that the grace of God is sufficient, as He said, but I also learned that grace is not an anesthetic. The hours and days—and even months—that followed Ned's death were so intense with pain that, looking back, I wonder that we did not die. The hurt was so great, the suffering so extreme, that I am amazed that the human frame, frail as it is, can survive such a blast. And I believe it was only possible by the grace of God.

"All thy waves and thy billows are gone over me" (Psalm 42:7). When beside that funeral home my heart suddenly turned gray with gloom, there was breathed the words "Ned is with the Lord." My heart broke; my spirit died within me. It was as though a mighty wound deep inside my being opened like a yawning cave and into its gaping mouth poured pain as white-hot as molten metal. But God was there. And as my fainting faith looked up to Him, the searing pain from that chastening rod became the softened stroke of the breath of His love, and suddenly there was peace. "When thou passest through the waters, I will be with thee; and through the rivers, they shall not overflow thee: when thou walkest through the fire, thou shalt not be burned; neither shall the flame kindle upon thee" (Isaiah 43:2). In the furnace of our affliction, as the flames leaped high and hot, there walked One as the Son of God, and we were not consumed. That is grace—God's grace. Full, glorious, true—promised in His Word, provided in His life, and constantly available to any trusting child. That grace is sufficient for you.

Seven

I BEGAN TO LEARN . . .

the greatness of the love of God. God is love, and therefore anything that emanates from Him has love as its source. No thought can come from God but that it be encased in love. No act can ever be culminated except God on the throne laid its plans in love. Love surrounds every principle that God puts forth for life. Love permeates every breath God breathes upon His creatures. Love is eternal; therefore it never changes. Love is complete; therefore it takes in everything. No circumstance can go beyond the love of God or find itself without the realm of His abode. God so loved the world that He gave His only Son; God commended His love to us in that while we were yet sinners Christ died for us; God loves us with an everlasting love, and it is that love that traced through all its history the plan that brought redemption to the souls of men. Love foreordained that Christ should die, and it was love that made the Father lead His beloved Son to Calvary and let Him die. The Father forsook the Son so that His love might never forsake us.

As we began to taste in all its sweetness the love of God in the hour of Ned's sudden death, somehow the bigness of it became overwhelming. God loved Ned—far more than we could ever do. He gave him to us in the first place; and in the giving He made him so winsome, sweet, and loving that every moment he was ours was one of joy. He let us have him for nearly sixteen years, and in those years He permitted us to see His own transforming work lay hold of every part of Ned's life. Then suddenly—before Ned was involved in anything or with anyone to whom his death might be too complicated, too confusing—God quickly took him home. Why do I think love did that? Simply because God is love, and He can act in no other way.

There are wars and rumors of wars today, all caused by the selfish sinfulness of unregenerated man. Has God's great love spared Ned in that respect? Sickness and disease is prevalent. Has Ned been kept from some long, lasting illness? There is sin today throughout the world, so dark and devastating in its effect that only those who keep themselves close, close to Christ escape its awful pull. Has Ned been kept from some dread act or scene?

Oh, love of God, Thou hast traced the course of this event, and Thou hast placed above each sad detail, to mark it for Thine own, a banner that is love.

Eight

I LEARNED . . .

that as we embrace the will of God, we find it sweet; and as we take up this cross to bear it for the Lord, we are enabled, by His grace, to plant our lilies at His feet. Before the words that told Ned's death had sounded their finale in our ears, we let our spirits bow before the Lord and say with hushed but real assurance, "Thank You, Lord, for this."

To be able to do that was a miracle. It is God's doing and even in my own eyes marvelous. God laid His hand quite suddenly—and certainly heavily—upon us that day. We had no warning that would prepare us. We could not see a reason; we could not find a cause. But we could trust the Doer, and we knelt and told Him so. As we repeated the words that were our sacrifice of praise, our beings reached out to the Lord who does all things well, and we were able to say, "Naked came I out of my mother's womb, and naked shall I return thither:

the Lord gave, and the Lord hath taken away; blessed be the name of the Lord." As we said that with our lips and experienced it with our hearts, we were not offended in Him.

The control of the universe is in the hand of a sovereign God, and from that hand comes no permissive will or second cause. This is a sovereign hand that does the sovereign will of a sovereign God. The hairs of our heads are numbered. A sparrow does not fall to the ground without God's notice. No power could have wrenched the life of our son from this earth had God not wanted it so; and my heart can only say, "Thy will be done."

Nine

I LEARNED . . .

that the sting of death is sin, and where sin has been forever dealt with at the Cross, the sting of death is gone. The sorrow of death remains; the separation of death is real and hard to bear, for all our being's natural love and desire remain for the one who has gone through the gates of death. However, to know to what that one has gone—rather, to whom that one has gone—removes forever all bite or awful wound that comes from doubt, uncertainty, or fear. No cost can be too great, no sacrifice of self too demanding, to find that glorious fact true when death comes stalking toward the one you love. May God in mercy make you see the Lamb of God who taketh away the sin of the world, so that when near an open grave you stand, you can look up and say with heartfelt certainty, "Thanks be to God, which giveth us the victory through our Lord Jesus Christ" (1 Corinthians 15:57).

Ten

I LEARNED . . .

that to contemplate heaven is to find great glory for one's soul. I believe that among the deepest desires of a Christian parent's heart lies one more important than all others. That desire is to see his or her child walk close to the Lord on earth and then brought at last to heaven's door and bidden by Jesus to enter in. From Ned's most early hour, my hope was firmly fixed upon God's covenant promise to the household of faith, and I trusted that the Lord would bring Ned to a knowledge of salvation so that he might one day be in glory. The fact that God fulfilled that promise sooner than we had anticipated does not alter the fact that He fulfilled the promise. It does not change the desire of our hearts that Ned be there. He is there, and the Lord Jesus is there, and where the Savior exists is heaven. "Absent from the body, . . . present with the Lord" (2 Corinthians 5:8). There is no sorrow there; no voice of weeping is heard in that land.

There is no need of light, for Jesus is the Light, and in Him is no darkness at all. There is joy in heaven and all that satisfies. Only righteousness prevails, and love that is perfect, and friendship that is true. No broken hopes or disappointments come within those courts, and God is all the glory.

Somehow, the reality of heaven and what it must be like to be there fills my heart with longing wonder and with gratitude for this that He has prepared for them that love Him.

Underlined in Ned's Bible are these verses: "In my Father's house are many mansions: if it were not so, I would have told you. I go to prepare a place for you. And if I go and prepare a place for you, I will come again, and receive you unto myself; that where I am, there ye may be also" (John 14:2–3).

My heart praises You, Lord Jesus, for who You are, and what You are, and for all You in Your mercy have wrought in our behalf.

Eleven

I LEARNED . . .

to rest in the full meaning of this Word from God: "Jesus Christ the same yesterday, and to day, and for ever" (Hebrews 13:8). I learned to think upon the constancy of Christ—the eternal unchangeableness of our Lord Jesus—who is the same yesterday and today and forever.

In the late afternoon of a day next to the last in several weeks of a happy family holiday, suddenly everything changed. Our hearts, our minds, our hopes, our home, our future, our plans, our present —all were changed. One moment Ned, our dearly beloved—tall, straight, full of life, full of fun, full of all the expectancy of youth—stood in the surf casting for fish, of which he laughingly promised me an abundance for supper. Hours later his body lay in a funeral parlor. Change? Never was there more sudden or certain change. It was as though the whole earth changed. Our beings rocked and reeled before the change, and it seemed as if some horrible explosion shook the foundations of the world. It was a change so quick, so final, so devastating, that our senses failed beneath the blow.

But there was one unchanging fact, one unalterable certainty: Jesus Christ was the same. Yesterday He had died for us. Yesterday His power had availed for us. Yesterday He had loved us with an everlasting love. Was there anything different about Him today? Was He changed? Had time altered Him? From 4:00 to 5:00 P.M. on that strange afternoon, did the eternity of God vary? How gloriously quieting to look up to our Lord and by faith find Him as He was before. Nothing different—His love everlasting, His availability ready, His power active, His grace sufficient, His peace perfect. As He was yesterday, He is today, and so He will remain for every day.

Twelve

I LEARNED . . .

to comprehend to a small degree the utter helplessness of man. How completely weak we are—how frail, how inadequate. Apart from God we cannot do anything, be anything, or accomplish anything. We are totally, thoroughly ineffective, and only as the triune God—Father, Son, and Holy Spirit—works in our behalf are we able to live and move and exist.

Ned's father and I, his sister and brother, and even many of our friends would have given all we have—even our lives—if we could have changed the events of that day, with Ned the helpless victim of a so-called accident, ourselves the startled victims of a deep heart-sorrow. But there was nothing anyone could do. The decrees of God had brought to pass what happened on that day; all the skills, the plans, the power, and the purposes that man could muster could not avail against the will of God, to change one thing that had occurred.

I am saying that not because we rebelled against the will of God. We accepted it that day; we accept it now. We do more than accept it. We rejoice in it and thank Him for it. But what I do long to say and have people believe is that life is fragile, and humans cannot change its length or its strength. We are living in a day when people are failing to accept the existence of God. This is an age of great achievement. Man is boasting in his own abilities: atomic energy, scientific discovery, electronic control, mechanical precision, and so on. But man is godless in his attitude toward those things. He fails to recognize or even think upon the absolute truth that what he has learned has been given him of God; for what he has accomplished he has been empowered of God; and those things he sees as large are in God's sight quite small.

Man is a total loss apart from God. And though he vaunts himself and becomes puffed up with his own size and importance, there lies before each one a time of reckoning that will come inevitably and surely, and no one can sidestep or evade its issues. The control of life and of death remains in the hand of God, and He will keep it so. Let men pound their fists and shout their defiances. We still come from God, and we still go to God. This is our beginning and our ending, and God in sovereign mercy and with infinite wisdom and power controls it all. We may not agree with this, but it remains true; and though all the winds of earth, all the howls of haughty hosts clamor against this truth, the truth remains. God created the heavens and the earth. He created the particles that form the atom that supplies the power that propels the mighty instruments that invade the skies and pierce the ocean's depth. God made man and breathed into him that which gives him life—that which is life. And when that life is over, it is over by God's will, and nothing anyone can do can change that fact. Man may blow his puny breath upon the acts of God; but all he does is assert himself for a little season, then he is gone.

I cannot help but believe that as God dips His greatness into our littleness, He dares us once again to bow and worship Him. He longs that we accept His mercy, believe His Word, and trust His grace. "The Lord . . . is longsuffering [toward us], not willing that any should perish, but that all should come to repentance" (2 Peter 3:9). He longs for us to say, "Thou art the Son of God" (Matthew 14:33).

For the Lord is a great God, and a great King above all gods. In his hand are the deep places of the earth: the strength of the hills is his also. The sea is his, and he made it: and his hands formed the dry land. O come, let us worship and bow down: let us kneel before the Lord our maker. (Psalm 95:3–6)

When God reaches into the stream of humanity and chooses to take from it someone for His purposes, He is no respecter of persons; He consults with no one in His plan. Our only hope at such an hour as this is to be in such relationship with Him that we can trust Him utterly and lean not to our own understanding. This God enabled us to do.

We had not expected Ned to die. He was so young, so full of life, so eager to live, so real in all his approaches, so vital to our own lives and happiness. I think we expect our parents to die, or our contemporaries—our sisters, brothers, friends. Somehow, when these are called home, we are saddened but not always surprised. Not so with Ned. I had not expected that in any way—and when I said, as we so often have with all of our children, "Lord, he is Yours. Take him for Your use. Do with him as You wish. I will not keep him for myself," I somehow had never thought of that possibility. I think I had always meant, "Lord, use his life," not, "Lord, take his life." But now God has taken his life, and Ned is gone, and all we have is a precious memory. All we have? No, we also have a precious hope. A blessed hope, foundational to the Christian life, and conditioned only on believing the Word of God.

> *For if we believe that Jesus died and rose again, even so God will bring with Him those who sleep in Jesus. For this we say to you by the word of the Lord, that we who are alive and remain until the coming of the Lord will by no means precede those who are asleep. For the Lord Himself will descend from heaven with a shout, with the voice of an archangel, and with the trumpet of God. And the dead in Christ will rise first. Then we who are alive and remain shall be caught up together with them in the clouds to meet the Lord in the air. And thus we shall always be with the Lord. Therefore comfort one another with these words.* (1 Thessalonians 4:14–18 NKJV)

We believe this truth and rejoice in all its promise to our hearts. In a little while we will be together again, and so shall we ever be with the Lord! I wish you would join us there by trusting Christ for all your need.

Part Two

NED

One

IT WAS NO VAGUE THING
that brought comfort to us when Ned died.
God brought the peace that passes understanding.
The reason for the hope that lies within us is not
given in a moment. There lay beyond the opening
of this grave a spiritual biography that I would like
to tell you, with the earnest prayer that you will
follow all the way.

Ned's life has a personal message for you.

If you are a parent and God has entrusted to
your care some precious child to lead—then do
not hesitate in leading him in the way everlasting.
You must not look to time to bring the needed
knowledge of salvation. You must not depend on
future hours in which to chart the course that
leads us to the Savior. Time may be running out;
and when that last second of life's appointed hour
has spent itself, there is no turning back. The door
of death is merciless in its finality. You cannot
snatch even one precious second to say the thing

you wish you had said or do the thing you wish you had done. You cannot reassess your values then, or change the course of those events that careless unconcern or worldly attitude allowed to rise. When God calls your loved one home, He simply takes him in and closes the door, and that is that. Weep as you will, love as you cannot help but love, long as you long; there is not one word that you can say, one thing that you can do to make anything different. "To day if ye will hear his voice, harden not your heart" (Psalm 95:7–8).

The first thing that you must be sure of, to know the peace of God in the hour of death, is your own relationship to Christ. Have you ever really become a Christian? Have you with simple childlike faith forsaken all you are and taken Christ? Have you believed what He said?

I am the light of the world: he that followeth me shall not walk in darkness, but shall have the light of life. (John 8:12)

I am the door: by me if any man enter in, he shall be saved, and shall go in and out, and find pasture. (John 10:9)

Neither is there salvation in any other: for there is none other name under heaven given among men, whereby we must be saved. (Acts 4:12)

That if thou shalt confess with thy mouth the Lord Jesus, and shalt believe in thine heart that God hath raised him from the dead, thou shalt be saved. (Romans 10:9)

And it shall come to pass, that whosoever shall call on the name of the Lord shall be saved. (Acts 2:21)

For God so loved the world, that he gave his only begotten Son, that whosoever believeth in him should not perish, but have everlasting life. For God sent not his Son into the world to condemn the world; but that the world through him might be saved. He that believeth on him is not condemned: but he that believeth not is condemned already, because he hath not believed in the name of the only begotten Son of God. (John 3:16–18)

You do not have to know a lot of things to become a child of God. You only have to know a person and, knowing Him, you have to recognize your own need as a guilty, lost sinner. And as you know this, you must repent and come to this person, Jesus Christ the Son of God, and take Him as your Savior and your Lord. The blood of Christ was freely poured out for us all on Calvary, and it avails for any trusting heart who will come and be cleansed.

Friend, whoever you are, wherever you are, if there is uncertainty in your heart today, take Jesus now and, in the taking, find peace and life everlasting.

Two

IF YOU ARE A CHRISTIAN

and are sure of your relationship to God, then as friend to friend and fellow believer, I would like to tell you more.

A choice confronts parents as they recognize their responsibility in the rearing of children. We stand at a point in the road in which there is a two-way fork. Down one fork, proud parental eyes behold a smooth, shining highway lined on either side with every beauty and every worldly sight and scene so lovely to our vision and so inviting to our minds. Down this road we can see ease, enjoyment, fame and fortune, social success, intellectual achievement—all waiting for those we love. This road winds and turns and invites each one of us to explore its enticing length.

The other road is straight and narrow, and along its edges we see no sunny glades or green-swathed hills. It looks difficult, and the way is steep. There is not even any promise of shade or a resting place. It is a road that begins to climb at its start, and it looks like a long, long way. However, if we look, we see beside this road a cross and One who on that cross provided everything we need to make the journey. The Lord Jesus Himself in all His power and beauty stands beside the road to welcome each newcomer and bid him hurry in the way. This way is a highway for God, and Jesus is the Way to it and the Way on it. He makes the crooked places straight, the rough places plain. And He, when we press our hands in His, will lead us every step up to the Father's house.

Perhaps you as a parent have hesitated and wished you could take both roads—the wide one for good times, when everything is easy and the days are glad and bright, and the other one when circumstances change, and all is not well, and you feel the need of help. If you are standing at this fork, halting between two opinions, do not tarry longer but choose God's road and, taking your family with you, go with the Lord Jesus.

To do that is to submit your will to the will of God for everything and in everything. That involves your child's early training. In his first years you must give him the security and the privilege of discipline. He must be taught to obey; he must be taught to love, not hate; he must be taught to live for God, not self.

Then you must yield your child's education to God that He might plan it for His glory and not for man's achievement. The mind with all its marvelous processes and all its ability and power is certainly one of God's greatest creations, and He intends that it be used to its full capacity. But in the process of filling the mind, though we might begin at God, if we then turn away from Him and take as every premise of thought those tenets that lead us down the avenue of worldly wisdom, as long as we hold in this direction we have no hope of ever coming back to that from which we once began. God is the beginning of wisdom. He is the continuation of wisdom. He is wisdom. His Word is truth—it is absolute truth—and to depart from it in search of truth will never lead us to the thing for which we search, since our course takes us from the source of that which we seek.

If you are socially ambitious for your child and are wishing you could have God *and* position, people, or things, then quickly tell God so and lay this at His feet. If your children run with the world, they will become as the world. If they taste earthly pleasures, they will reap earthly fruits. If they seek the pleasures of this world even for a season, recall that season follows season. Spring becomes summer, summer becomes fall, and suddenly it is winter, and the frosts have come to sear the leaf and dry the root, while howling winds break down each well-planned day; and only cold remains and deep, deep snow to bury beneath its load each faint hope of heaven. Moses by faith refused to be called the son of Pharaoh's daughter, choosing rather to suffer affliction with the people of God than to enjoy the pleasures of sin for a season. He esteemed the reproach of Christ greater riches than the treasures of Egypt.

But many say, and how often have I heard it, "I do not think it right to make the choices for my child. I think it only fair to let him grow up and then make his own choice. Why should I push the things I believe? Besides, if I do, I will drive him further away." A feeble defense from a feeble heart that holds a feeble faith. A practical atheism. God does not mock us with His promises or fail to meet the conditions of His eternal covenant. If we fulfill our responsibility regarding those He gives us as our own, we need not fear God will fail in His.

The reasoning that tells us to let our youngsters make their own spiritual choices fails at every point. Would we be counted wise or kind and worthy parents, were we to let our little ones choose their own course of safety in the matter of physical things? Are we to let them wander in a vast wilderness quite unattended until they lose their way? Or should we watch them face a danger and not lead them away from what spells disaster? The fire that burns, the knife that cuts, the poisoned food, or fatal drink—are we not quick to show a little child all those perils? Should we not all the more lead their souls away from sin to those eternal choices that will keep them for the Lord and let them enter heaven's gates to dwell with Him? If there had been one small doubt within my heart that day when God took Ned home—one doubt concerning his salvation and his acceptance at the throne, I believe my soul would have died within me. But by the grace of God and through a sure knowledge of His Word, we knew whom we and Ned had believed and we were assured that He would keep that which we had committed to Him against that day.

At this point, it was faith alone that kept my heart regarding the way in which Ned died.

Without faith the inevitable questions would come. Had we failed? Were we guilty in allowing Ned to drive? But by faith the inevitable answer stayed our hearts and held our minds. God had led us and him every step that brought us to this hour and this place in our lives. God had not failed.

Three

NED

was just like any boy his age.

He looked the part, dressed the part, and talked the part of any sixteen-year-old. And yet he wasn't just like all the rest. He was to those who knew him different enough to make a difference—a difference that was radical and counted for everything. For Ned belonged to Christ, and Christ belonged to him. In every area of his being, the Lord claimed him for His own. Ned's eyes were bright because his heart was pure. His mind was keen because his heart was fixed. His body was straight and strong because his heart was kept. And his soul was safe, because his life belonged to God.

It was not always so. When he was small, his willful self was in control and the "I wants" and "I wills" of his desires were evident. But one day that changed. Up until that time as we had taught him and showed him and helped him, he had known about the Lord and had spoken of Jesus as being in his heart. He had prayed his childish prayers and learned his Bible verses, and to all appearances he knew and loved the Lord Jesus.

However, when he was not quite five an illness struck him down, and for several weeks he was severely sick. Toward the close of the serious time when there was beginning the long, slow process of nursing back his strength, one night I settled in to read and entertain through every avenue of my imagination until the hours would pass and he would safely be asleep. Somehow, no story came, and nothing stirred my tongue to fable or to song. So I climbed on the big four-poster bed with him, propped upon the pillows by his side, and took the Bible and a children's Bible storybook and began to trace through its thrilling history the story of redemption. Beginning "in the beginning" and speaking in language adequate to a young child's need, I showed Ned the ways of God as He has charted out the course of man since his beginning until now and on into the future of His eternal plan.

When I had finished on that glorious note of Christ's return to earth when He will come again to receive us to Himself, Ned quietly said, "Mother, tell me that all again."

"Do you mean all that I have told you, you want me to tell again?"

"Yes, Mama, tell me it all again." And so I did. A long story—an old story. But it rang new that night. For as I came again, quite late in the evening, to the part about Jesus coming back again, Ned said so gently, "If Jesus came tonight, would He take me to heaven?"

Glorious grace of God that made it possible for me to know the answer; for I simply said, "If you have taken Jesus into your heart and are trusting Him as your Savior, He will take you to heaven. Otherwise, He will not, for only those who believe on Him as their Savior and their Lord are His. Have you taken Him into your heart?"

"I am not sure."

"Would you like to?"

"Yes."

We prayed on our knees up in the big old bed, and Ned asked the Lord Jesus to come into his heart and save him. And He did.

Almost immediately there was a change. He became a new creation, and the old things passed away. His temper that had so often crowded out his otherwise sunny disposition came under control, and his willfulness became obedience. His stubbornness became love. He went from being the most difficult child to manage to the easiest. And the days that made out the remaining short span of his life were filled with happiness and joy for him and for us.

When Ned was only seven, he raised his hand one night in a meeting in our church to say to the Lord that he wished to make public his profession that he belonged to Christ and went forward afterward in response to the call. When he was thirteen he stood in a missionary meeting to say that he would pray and seek the Lord's will regarding missionary service. And then in the final year of his life he yielded wholly to the Lord, declaring that he no longer wanted to live for himself but wanted Christ to have control of all his being and his service. He looked forward with real anticipation to someday serving God on the mission field, taking for his verse Philippians 1:21: "For to me to live is Christ, and to die is gain."

You may think that the course of his life was what it was because we forced him. Nothing could be further from the truth. We taught him all we knew about God, about righteous living, and about the joy and fruits of serving Christ. We taught him to obey us so that he might learn to obey God. We hedged him in at every point with the Word of God and the love of our hearts and told him yes when it would enlarge his life and no when what he wished would soil his soul or lead him to do something wrong. We walked with him through the details of self-discipline. And we showed him the way when his lack of wisdom made him unaware of the proper course. But where he could cope with them we left the choices all to him. We wanted no outward conformity, no puppet that gave a puny squeak when someone pulled his chain. We let him live his life and grow his soul and build his personality. We only tended him and nurtured him and held him to the better way.

He was a nonconformist from the start, and no friends ever pushed him to the point of their desire if he found it contrary to his way; and quite often he found himself alone and walking away from the crowd instead of with it. I recall so vividly Ned's response to the daily and inner questions of his early teen years. He would seek the shelter of his upstairs room. And there, propped on the foot of his bed with a battered cowboy hat on his head and his gaze fixed on the upper window through which he saw the sky and the trees and the clouds, he would strum his old guitar and sing, "Don't fence me in."

Well, he was not "fenced in" in his spirit. It was as free as the birds he loved to watch. And his heart and life were carefree in the security of the controlled atmosphere of the "fences of God." How gloriously comforting today to realize how utterly free he now will ever be.

He had so many friends. He made them easily and loved them dearly; but he always showed them how and where he stood, and many have told us of the effect of his life upon their lives.

A former high school teacher wrote:

I taught Ned algebra in the ninth grade and remember him as an exceptionally fine boy. On one occasion the question of plans for the future came up in class. His answer to the question, "What do you plan to do?" was, "I want to serve my Lord Jesus." Never before in my teaching experience did a pupil give an answer like that.

The headmaster of the Christian high school he later attended wrote:

We loved Ned because he was so lovable. His charming dignity and twinkle were his trademark. His growth in grace during this past year was very much in evidence. . . . I remember chatting with him one day in the infirmary about his grades. He turned with that soft smile of his and said, "I am going to make the honor roll with God's help." You know the results. He did. I am glad we had Ned here this year.

A missionary leader and friend wrote:

This past September it was my privilege to be in the fall conference. I had a good chat with Ned at that time. He seemed to be developing so nicely. There was such grace and ease in the way in which he greeted me and shared his thoughts. Then too, it was such a joy to note the way in which his heart had been opening to the Lord. His will was truly reaching out after the lordship of Christ. So filled with promise. So bright seemed the way before him.

A friend and former baby-sitter who had stayed with Ned and his brother when they were little wrote:

It is so often a trite saying about somebody's smile being the thing one will never forget, but I'm sure I'm not the first one who has mentioned what his smile meant. I saw him just a minute at graduation, and two things stood out in that minute on the side porch: first, how tall and handsome he was getting; and then, how his ready smile hadn't changed! . . . I remember when we would check to be sure Ned was all set for bed. Alongside his bed were lined up his tomahawk, his basketball, and his knotted rope that he had worked on learning the knots, I guess. Then we would all pray together, and all was well with the Fleece boys. They had committed their folks and the work of the Lord to Him, and they knew He was well able to hear and answer.

All of this is given to show the power of God applied to a young boy's life. It also shows that the plan of God does not of necessity take a long time to be fulfilled. God made Ned for purposes that could be finished on earth in sixteen years. In that time He gave to Ned all his needed abilities to accomplish all that was intended for his life. His personality was such that God used it in all its casual winsomeness to gladden many hearts. And though the loss to us is great, we are thankful that Jesus has that personality safe within His keeping now.

Four

NED'S CHIEF JOYS
were outdoor things. All his leisure time, and
often all his time, was spent in those pursuits that
took him to the woods and lakes—to ride, to fish,
to hunt.

Of all his interests, though, he loved baseball
the best. Before he entered school he knew by
heart the rating of every favored big-league player
in the news; and it seemed to us he learned to
read from the sports page baseball scores rather
than the first-grade reader. When he early joined
himself to the local Little League, he plugged away
with dogged determination to star at his second-
base position. When his team came up to their
opening game after weeks of hot, hard practice, on
Ned's first call up at bat he hit a home run. By the
time he rounded the field and came in over home
plate, he was a ball player from the heart. From
then on he practiced with all available time and
strength and dreamed deep, satisfying dreams of

someday making Big League. He slid into every base, he pulled nearly every ligament and sprained nearly every joint sometime during those years of practice, but he never gave up. He always came back for more.

He loved dogs, horses, boats, cars, and westerns —anything that had life and action. He learned to do so many things and to like so many people, and toward his friends his heart was warm and sympathetic.

He read everything and anything he could get his hands on. When he was still a little boy he'd pick up *Time* magazine along with the Our Gang Series, a biography of George Washington, a Boy Scout manual, and a nature study book to combine for an evening's reading.

However, always around and through those many interests ran a constant purpose of training toward the future—and with sly humor he would defend his often purely pleasurable pursuits as being necessary to the making of a man. He had quite completely given himself to God to go out in missionary service, and I think that from the natural viewpoint that was one of the puzzling things about his death. The need is great in the world today—the harvest is ready, and the laborers are few. Ned had half his battle won in that respect. He loved the Lord, he loved people—all kinds of people —and he wanted with all his heart to serve them both in some place of God's choosing and for God's glory.

Ned's life on earth only lasted a little while in the great reach of eternity, but the shortness of his life taught me many things. One thing it showed me is that time in quantity is not always necessary to produce what God intends. It is not how much of time we have with which to do, but how much we do with what we have.

"Whosoever will save his life shall lose it; but whosoever shall lose his life for my sake and the gospel's, the same shall save it" (Mark 8:35).

Ned lost his life on earth so far as this world's gain or pleasure was concerned; and he planned to lose it for the Savior insofar as future service was concerned. But he saved his life by losing it, and when he so suddenly stood before the Lord Jesus that June afternoon, how glorious for him and for us that he had already relinquished himself to God. Nothing was different in the plan of God for Ned but the place of the plan's fulfillment. That place is heaven.

God's plan for the missionary outreach has not changed. He uses men and women to take the gospel out. His plan is still the same. But I wonder if He might not need someone to take Ned's place out on the firing line.

It could be there sits in some lonely place a weary soul for whom Christ died—someone who waits with haunting fear and knows no hope until the message comes. It may be God would use you in Ned's stead to sow the seed and plant the Word to fall into the ground and die. But if you die you will bring forth much fruit, and the Lord Jesus "shall see of the travail of his soul, and shall be satisfied" (Isaiah 53:11).

Will you not lose your life for Christ's sake and the gospel's and thereby save your life for God and eternity?

Beauty, Message, Ministry
Gift books from Moody

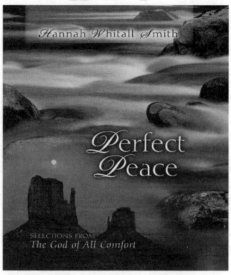

Selections from The God of All Comfort
Perfect Peace

Far from the abundant life offered in Scripture, many Christians live in fear, despair, and doubt. Perfect Peace is one of the few solid options on the market to give peace and comfort to Christians who are experiencing grief and lacking the hope found only through Jesus Christ. Through the perfect blend of Scripture, poetry, and beautiful scenery, it will bless and encourage those who are hurting.

Hardcover 0-8024-6692-3

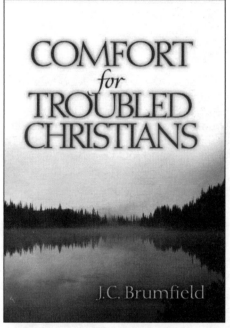